HAL•LEONARD

JAZZ PLAY-ALONG®

Book and CD for Bb, Eb, C and Bass Clef Instruments

volume 126

Arranged and Produced by Mark Taylor

Count Basie CLASSICS

10 FAVORITE STANDARDS

BOOK

CD

Photo by William "PoPsie" Randolph
www.PoPsiePhotos.com

ISBN 978-1-4234-6868-4

HAL•LEONARD® CORPORATION

7777 W. BLUEMOUND RD. P.O. BOX 13819 MILWAUKEE, WI 53213

Visit Hal Leonard Online at
www.halleonard.com

COUNT BASIE CLASSICS

Volume 126

Arranged and Produced by
Mark Taylor

Featured Players:

Graham Breedlove–Trumpet
John Desalme–Tenor Sax
Tony Nalker–Piano
Jim Roberts–Guitar and Bass
Chuck Redd–Drums

Recorded at Bias Studios, Springfield, Virginia
Bob Dawson, Engineer

HOW TO USE THE CD:

Each song has <u>two</u> tracks:

1) Split Track/Melody

Woodwind, Brass, Keyboard, and **Mallet Players** can use this track as a learning tool for melody style and inflection.

Bass Players can learn and perform with this track – remove the recorded bass track by turning down the volume on the LEFT channel.

Keyboard and **Guitar Players** can learn and perform with this track – remove the recorded piano part by turning down the volume on the RIGHT channel.

2) Full Stereo Track

Soloists or **Groups** can learn and perform with this accompaniment track with the RHYTHM SECTION only.

I NEVER KNEW

WORDS BY GUS KAHN
MUSIC BY TED FIORITO

SOLOS (4 CHORUSES)

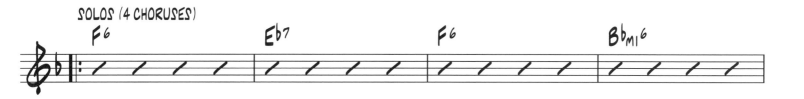

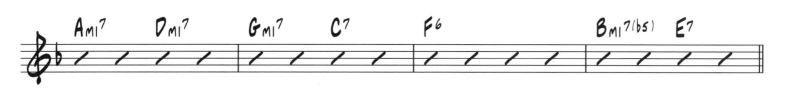

D.S. AL CODA
TAKE REPEAT

KANSAS CITY

WORDS AND MUSIC BY JERRY LEIBER
AND MIKE STOLLER

C VERSION

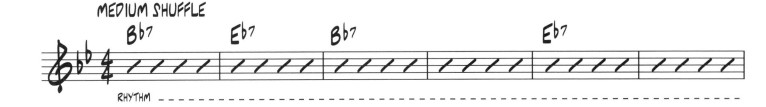

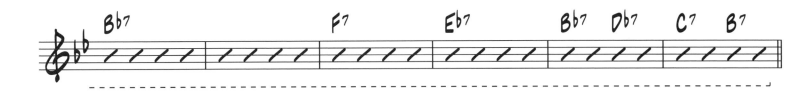

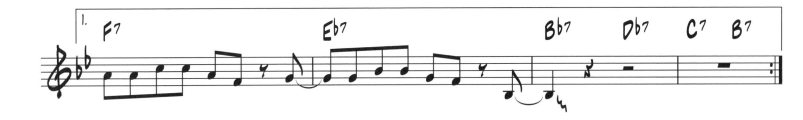

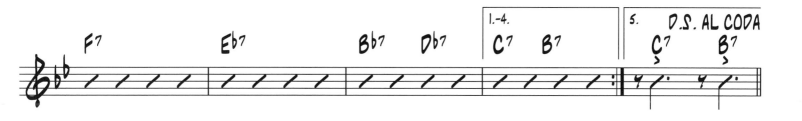

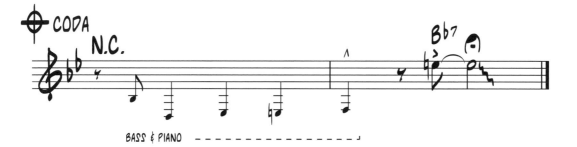

MOON RIVER
FROM THE PARAMOUNT PICTURE BREAKFAST AT TIFFANY'S

WORDS BY JOHNNY MERCER
MUSIC BY HENRY MANCINI

MOONLIGHT BECOMES YOU
FROM THE PARAMOUNT PICTURE ROAD TO MOROCCO

WORDS BY JOHNNY BURKE
MUSIC BY JAMES VAN HEUSEN

CD
7 : SPLIT TRACK/MELODY
8 : FULL STEREO TRACK

C VERSION

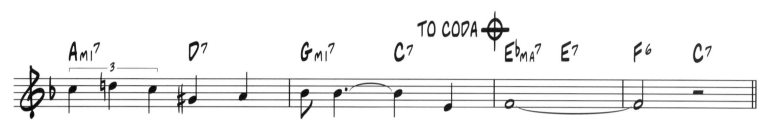

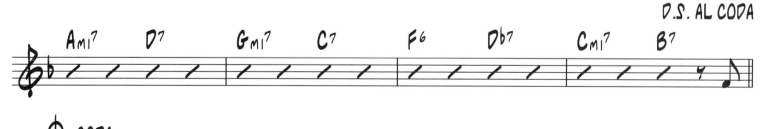

ON THE SUNNY SIDE OF THE STREET

CD
9 : SPLIT TRACK/MELODY
10 : FULL STEREO TRACK

LYRIC BY DOROTHY FIELDS
MUSIC BY JIMMY MCHUGH

C VERSION

SOLO

D.S. AL CODA

CODA

CD

11 : SPLIT TRACK/MELODY
12 : FULL STEREO TRACK

C VERSION

ONE MINT JULEP

WORDS AND MUSIC BY
RUDOLPH TOOMBS

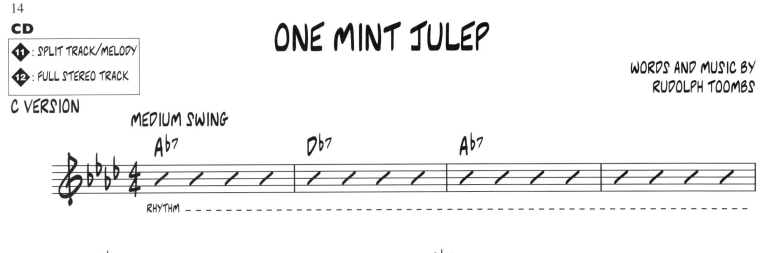

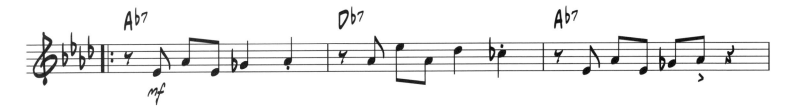

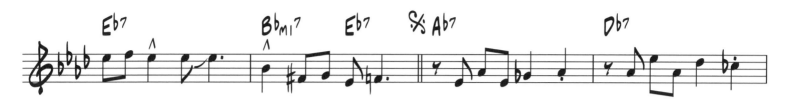

POLKA DOTS AND MOONBEAMS

CD
13 : SPLIT TRACK/MELODY
14 : FULL STEREO TRACK

C VERSION

WORDS BY JOHNNY BURKE
MUSIC BY JIMMY VAN HEUSEN

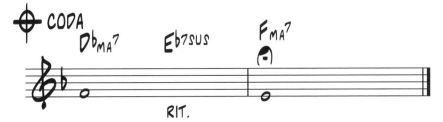

SHE'S FUNNY THAT WAY

WORDS BY RICHARD A. WHITING
MUSIC BY NEIL MORET

CD
🔷15 : SPLIT TRACK/MELODY
🔷16 : FULL STEREO TRACK

C VERSION

TEACH ME TONIGHT

WORDS BY SAMMY CAHN
MUSIC BY GENE DEPAUL

CD
- **17** : SPLIT TRACK/MELODY
- **18** : FULL STEREO TRACK

C VERSION

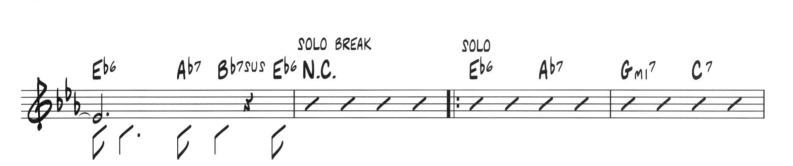

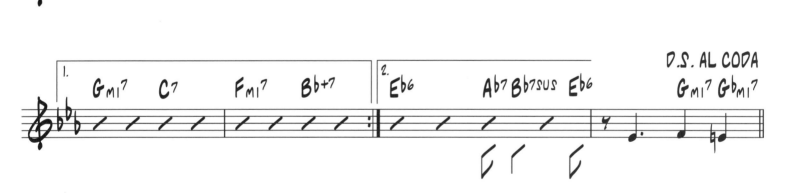

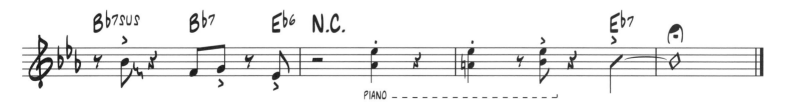

These Foolish Things
(Remind Me of You)

WORDS BY HOLT MARVELL
MUSIC BY JACK STRACHEY

CD
19 : SPLIT TRACK/MELODY
20 : FULL STEREO TRACK

C VERSION

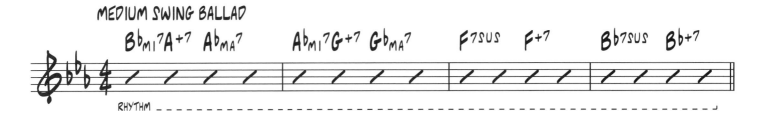

I NEVER KNEW

WORDS BY GUS KAHN
MUSIC BY TED FIORITO

Bb VERSION

SOLOS (4 CHORUSES)

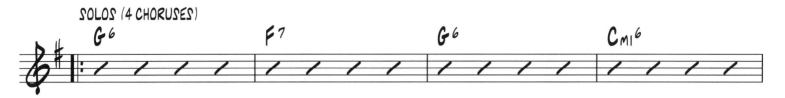

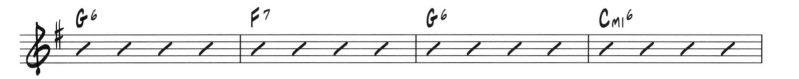

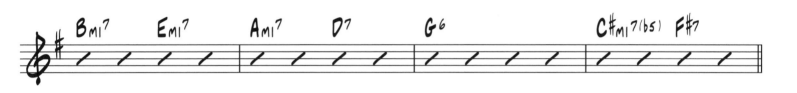

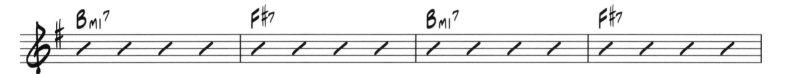

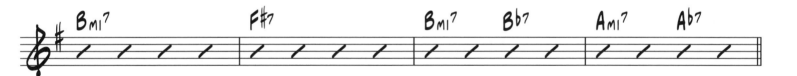

D.S. AL CODA
TAKE REPEAT

KANSAS CITY

Bb VERSION

WORDS AND MUSIC BY JERRY LEIBER
AND MIKE STOLLER

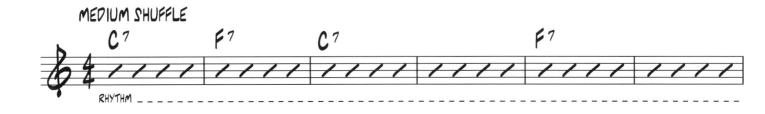

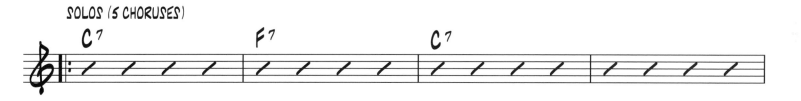

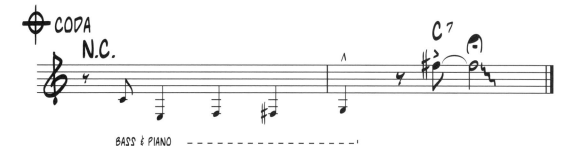

CD

5 : SPLIT TRACK/MELODY
6 : FULL STEREO TRACK

Bb VERSION

MOON RIVER
FROM THE PARAMOUNT PICTURE BREAKFAST AT TIFFANY'S

WORDS BY JOHNNY MERCER
MUSIC BY HENRY MANCINI

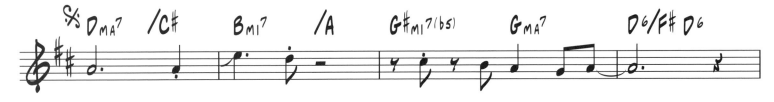

Bb VERSION

MOONLIGHT BECOMES YOU

FROM THE PARAMOUNT PICTURE ROAD TO MOROCCO

WORDS BY JOHNNY BURKE
MUSIC BY JAMES VAN HEUSEN

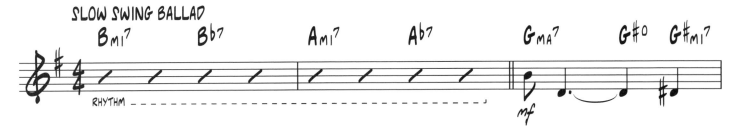

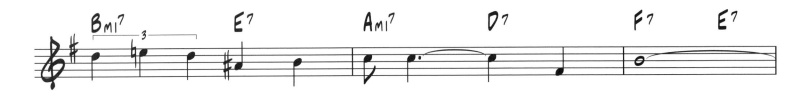

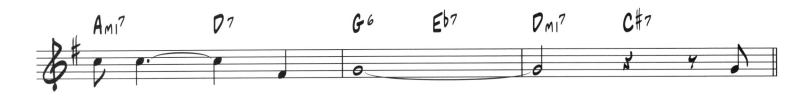

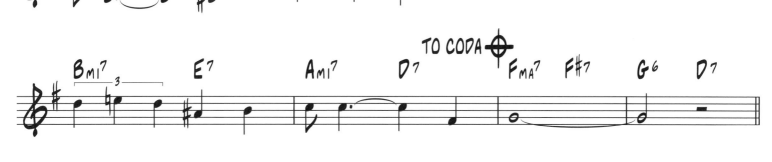

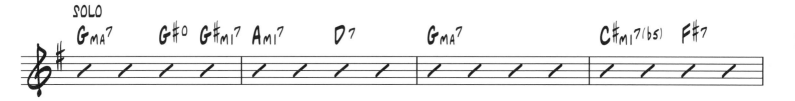

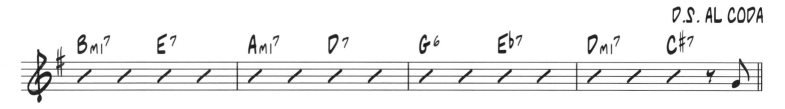

ON THE SUNNY SIDE OF THE STREET

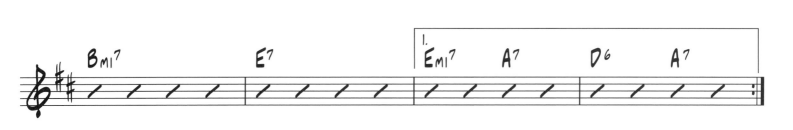

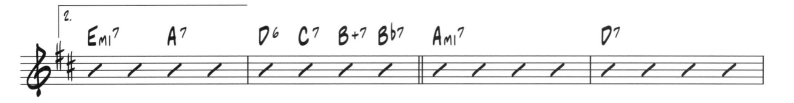

One Mint Julep

WORDS AND MUSIC BY
RUDOLPH TOOMBS

Bb VERSION

MEDIUM SWING

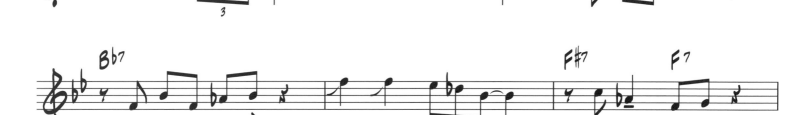

CD

13 : SPLIT TRACK/MELODY
14 : FULL STEREO TRACK

POLKA DOTS AND MOONBEAMS

WORDS BY JOHNNY BURKE
MUSIC BY JIMMY VAN HEUSEN

Bb VERSION

MEDIUM SWING BALLAD

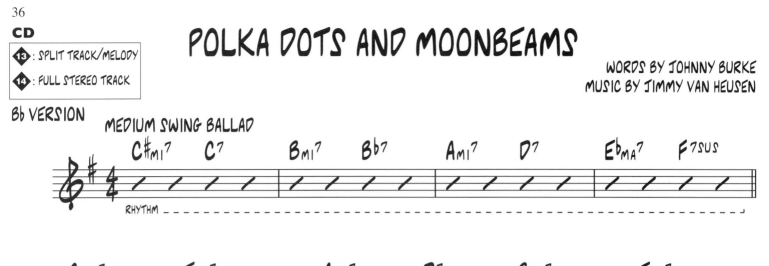

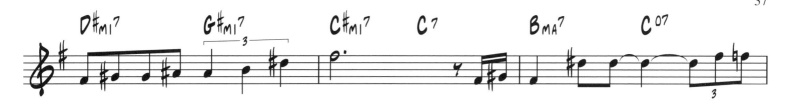

SHE'S FUNNY THAT WAY

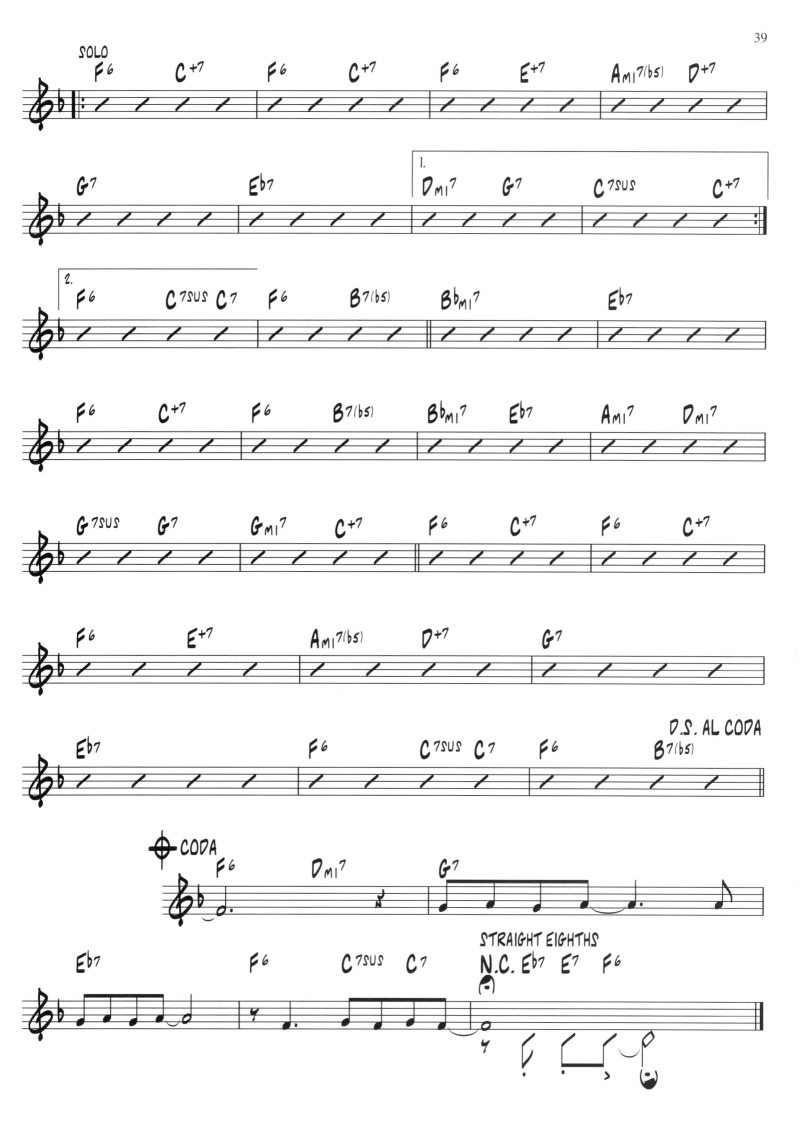

Teach Me Tonight

CD

17 : SPLIT TRACK/MELODY
18 : FULL STEREO TRACK

WORDS BY SAMMY CAHN
MUSIC BY GENE DEPAUL

Bb VERSION

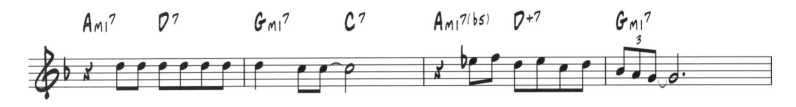

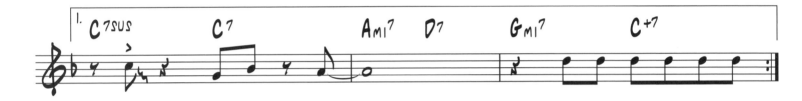

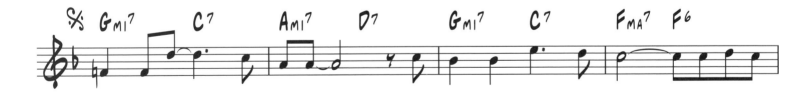

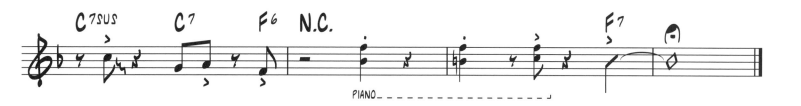

These Foolish Things
(Remind Me of You)

WORDS BY HOLT MARVELL
MUSIC BY JACK STRACHEY

CD
19 : SPLIT TRACK/MELODY
20 : FULL STEREO TRACK

Bb VERSION

MEDIUM SWING BALLAD

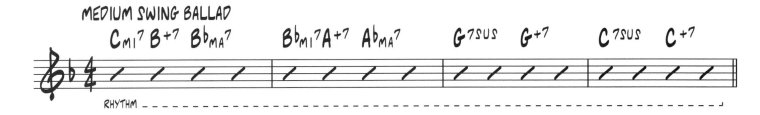

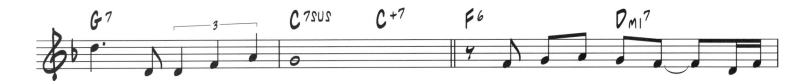

I NEVER KNEW

WORDS BY GUS KAHN
MUSIC BY TED FIORITO

Eb VERSION

SOLOS (4 CHORUSES)

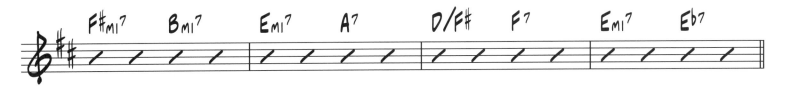

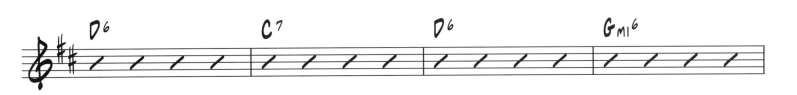

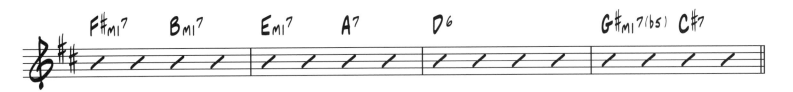

D.S. AL CODA
TAKE REPEAT

PIANO *8VB*

KANSAS CITY

WORDS AND MUSIC BY JERRY LEIBER
AND MIKE STOLLER

Eb VERSION

MEDIUM SHUFFLE

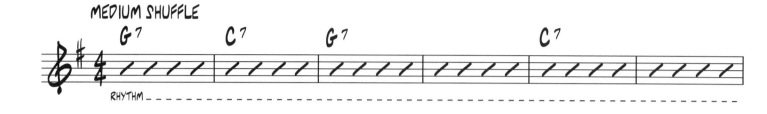

CD
⑤ : SPLIT TRACK/MELODY
⑥ : FULL STEREO TRACK

MOON RIVER

FROM THE PARAMOUNT PICTURE BREAKFAST AT TIFFANY'S

WORDS BY JOHNNY MERCER
MUSIC BY HENRY MANCINI

Eb VERSION

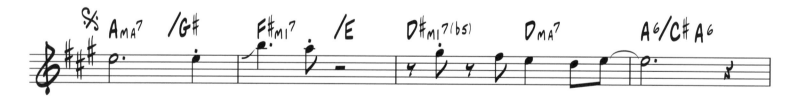

MOONLIGHT BECOMES YOU
FROM THE PARAMOUNT PICTURE ROAD TO MOROCCO

WORDS BY JOHNNY BURKE
MUSIC BY JAMES VAN HEUSEN

Eb VERSION

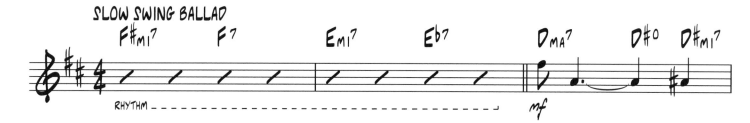

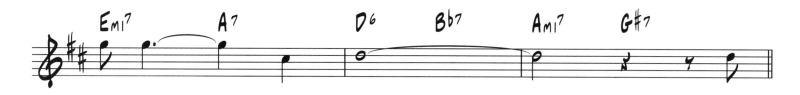

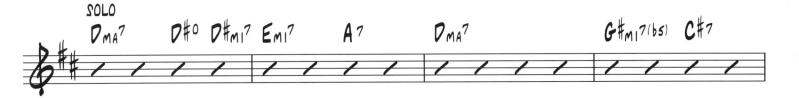

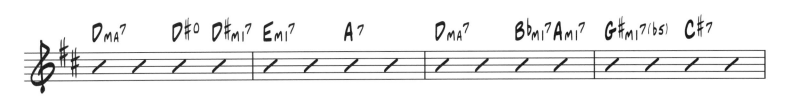

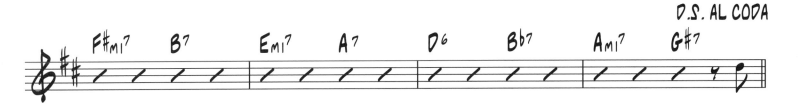

On the Sunny Side of the Street

CD
9 : SPLIT TRACK/MELODY
10 : FULL STEREO TRACK

LYRIC BY DOROTHY FIELDS
MUSIC BY JIMMY McHUGH

Eb VERSION

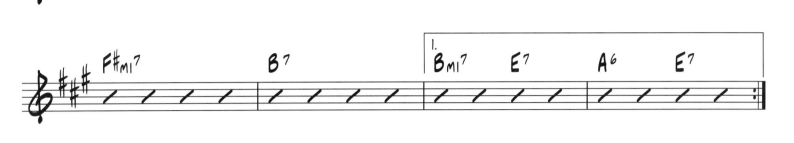

ONE MINT JULEP

CD
11 : SPLIT TRACK/MELODY
12 : FULL STEREO TRACK

WORDS AND MUSIC BY
RUDOLPH TOOMBS

Eb VERSION

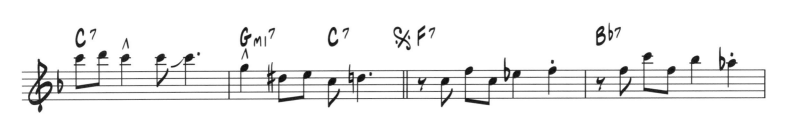

POLKA DOTS AND MOONBEAMS

WORDS BY JOHNNY BURKE
MUSIC BY JIMMY VAN HEUSEN

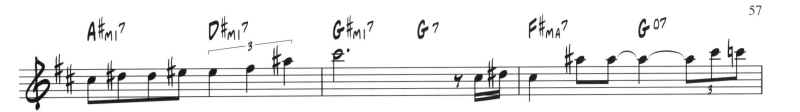

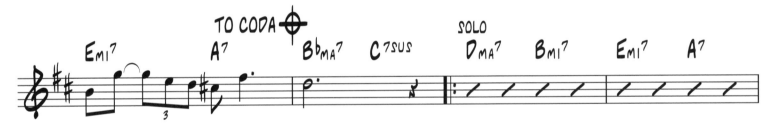

CD

15 : SPLIT TRACK/MELODY
16 : FULL STEREO TRACK

SHE'S FUNNY THAT WAY

WORDS BY RICHARD A. WHITING
MUSIC BY NEIL MORET

Eb VERSION

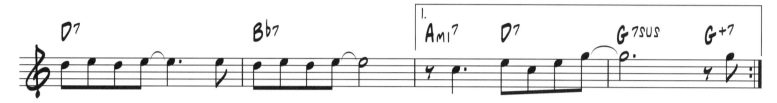

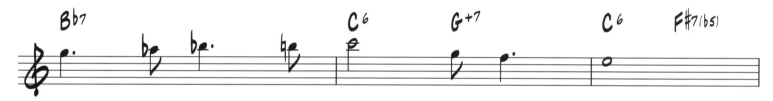

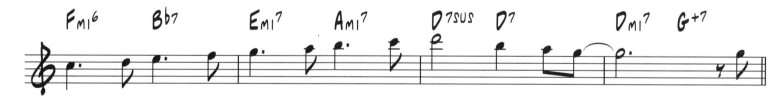

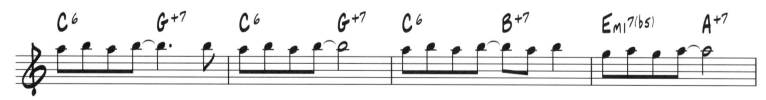

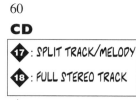

Teach Me Tonight

WORDS BY SAMMY CAHN
MUSIC BY GENE DEPAUL

Eb VERSION

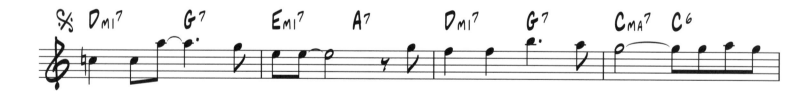

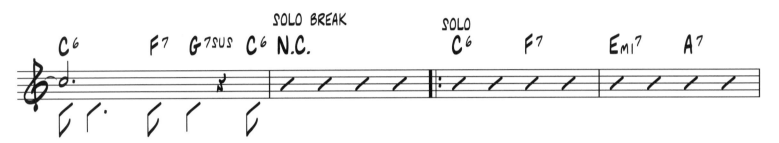

These Foolish Things
(Remind Me of You)

WORDS BY HOLT MARVELL
MUSIC BY JACK STRACHEY

Eb VERSION

I NEVER KNEW

WORDS BY GUS KAHN
MUSIC BY TED FIORITO

SOLOS (4 CHORUSES)

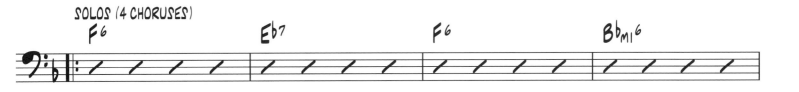

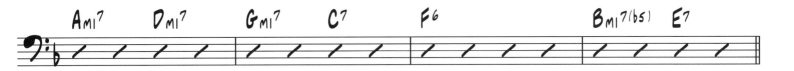

D.S. AL CODA
TAKE REPEAT

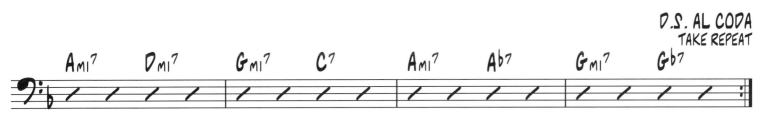

KANSAS CITY

WORDS AND MUSIC BY JERRY LEIBER
AND MIKE STOLLER

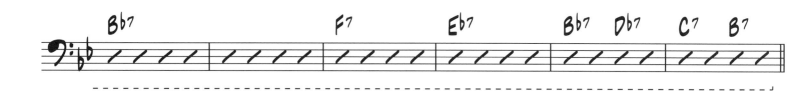

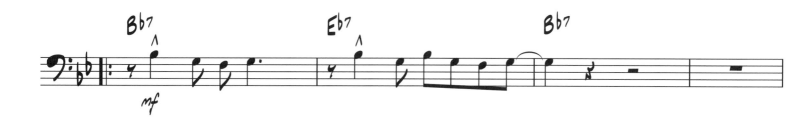

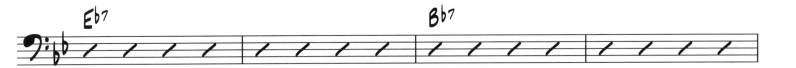

MOON RIVER

FROM THE PARAMOUNT PICTURE BREAKFAST AT TIFFANY'S

WORDS BY JOHNNY MERCER
MUSIC BY HENRY MANCINI

MOONLIGHT BECOMES YOU
FROM THE PARAMOUNT PICTURE ROAD TO MOROCCO

WORDS BY JOHNNY BURKE
MUSIC BY JAMES VAN HEUSEN

CD
7 : SPLIT TRACK/MELODY
8 : FULL STEREO TRACK

C VERSION

SLOW SWING BALLAD

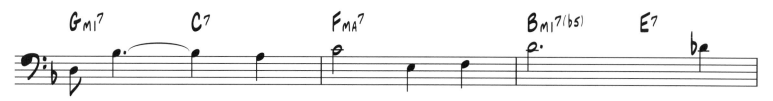

On the Sunny Side of the Street

LYRIC BY DOROTHY FIELDS
MUSIC BY JIMMY MCHUGH

CD

⬥11 : SPLIT TRACK/MELODY
⬥12 : FULL STEREO TRACK

ONE MINT JULEP

WORDS AND MUSIC BY
RUDOLPH TOOMBS

𝄢: C VERSION

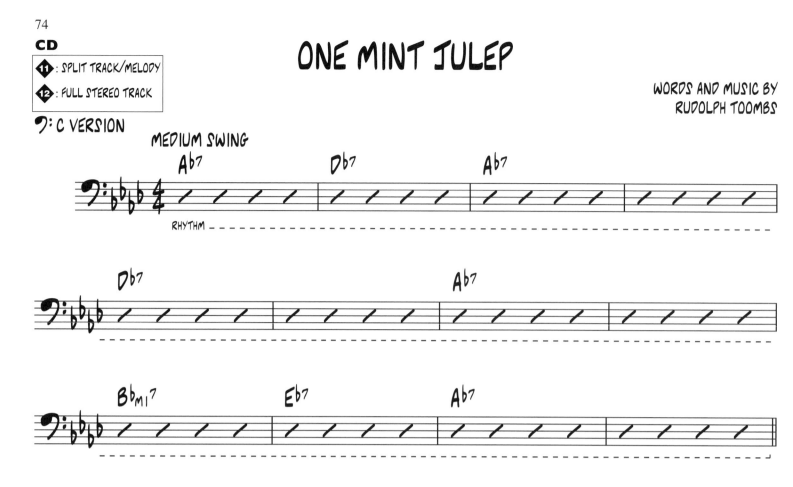

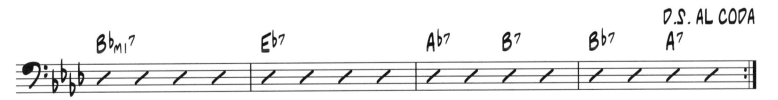

CD
13 : SPLIT TRACK/MELODY
14 : FULL STEREO TRACK

POLKA DOTS AND MOONBEAMS

WORDS BY JOHNNY BURKE
MUSIC BY JIMMY VAN HEUSEN

𝄢 : C VERSION

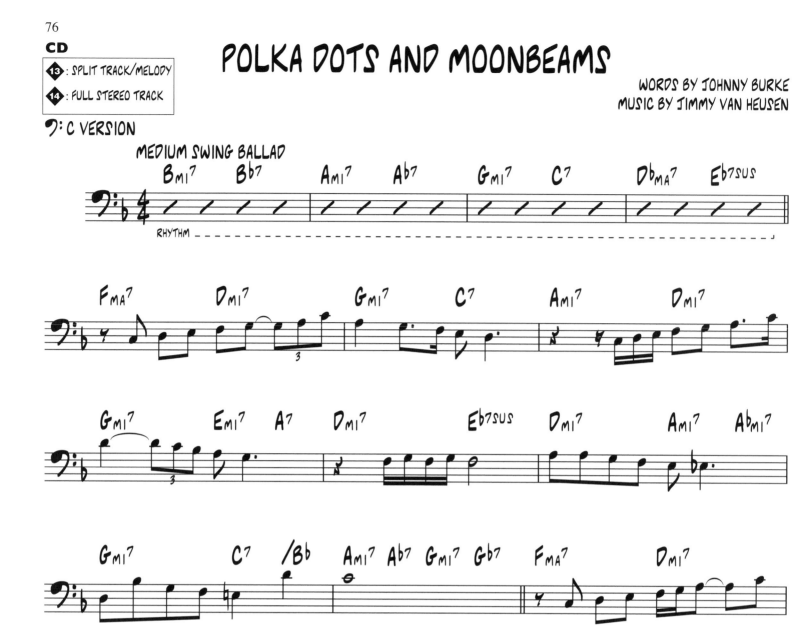

RIT.

SHE'S FUNNY THAT WAY

WORDS BY RICHARD A. WHITING
MUSIC BY NEIL MORET

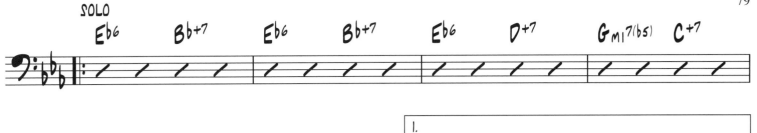

SOLO

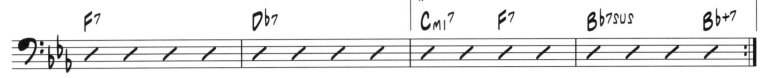

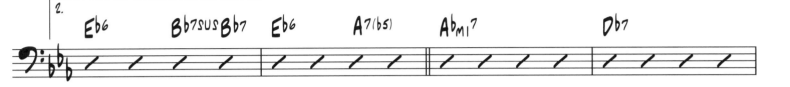

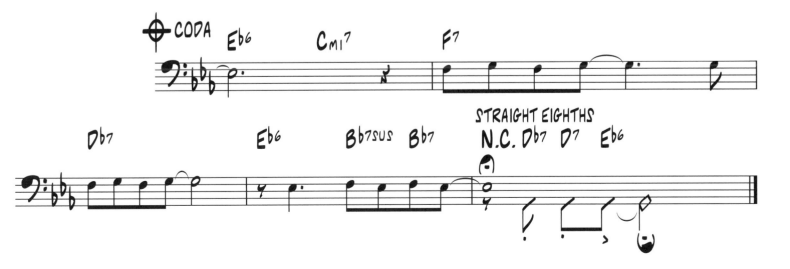

Teach Me Tonight

WORDS BY SAMMY CAHN
MUSIC BY GENE DEPAUL

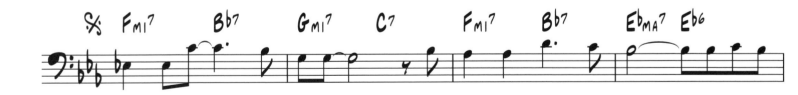

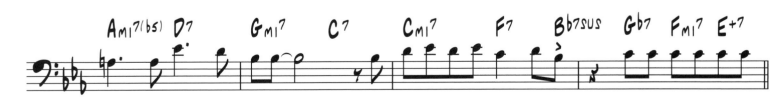

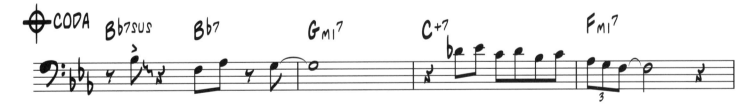

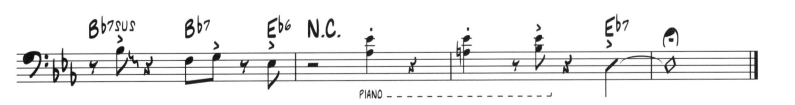

CD

◆19 : SPLIT TRACK/MELODY
◆20 : FULL STEREO TRACK

𝄢 C VERSION

These Foolish Things
(Remind Me of You)

WORDS BY HOLT MARVELL
MUSIC BY JACK STRACHEY

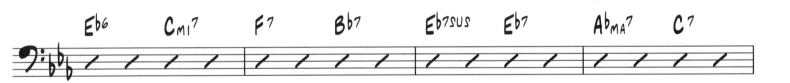

Jazz Instruction & Improvisation

Books for All Instruments from Hal Leonard

AN APPROACH TO JAZZ IMPROVISATION
by Dave Pozzi
Musicians Institute Press

INCLUDES TAB

Explore the styles of Charlie Parker, Sonny Rollins, Bud Powell and others with this comprehensive guide to jazz improvisation. Covers: scale choices • chord analysis • phrasing • melodies • harmonic progressions • more.
00695135 Book/CD Pack $17.95

BUILDING A JAZZ VOCABULARY
By Mike Steinel

A valuable resource for learning the basics of jazz from Mike Steinel of the University of North Texas. It covers: the basics of jazz • how to build effective solos • a comprehensive practice routine • and a jazz vocabulary of the masters.
00849911 ....$19.95

THE CYCLE OF FIFTHS
by Emile and Laura De Cosmo

This essential instruction book provides more than 450 exercises, including hundreds of melodic and rhythmic ideas. The book is designed to help improvisors master the cycle of fifths, one of the primary progressions in music. Guaranteed to refine technique, enhance improvisational fluency, and improve sight-reading!
00311114 ....$16.99

THE DIATONIC CYCLE
by Emile and Laura De Cosmo

Renowned jazz educators Emile and Laura De Cosmo provide more than 300 exercises to help improvisors tackle one of music's most common progressions: the diatonic cycle. This book is guaranteed to refine technique, enhance improvisational fluency, and improve sight-reading!
00311115 ....$16.95

EAR TRAINING
by Keith Wyatt,
Carl Schroeder and Joe Elliott
Musicians Institute Press

Covers: basic pitch matching • singing major and minor scales • identifying intervals • transcribing melodies and rhythm • identifying chords and progressions • seventh chords and the blues • modal interchange, chromaticism, modulation • and more.
00695198 Book/2-CD Pack...................................$24.95

EXERCISES AND ETUDES FOR THE JAZZ INSTRUMENTALIST
by J.J. Johnson

Designed as study material and playable by any instrument, these pieces run the gamut of the jazz experience, featuring common and uncommon time signatures and keys, and styles from ballads to funk. They are progressively graded so that both beginners and professionals will be challenged by the demands of this wonderful music.
00842018 Bass Clef Edition....................................$16.95
00842042 Treble Clef Edition $16.95

JAZZOLOGY
THE ENCYCLOPEDIA OF JAZZ THEORY FOR ALL MUSICIANS
by Robert Rawlins and Nor Eddine Bahha

This comprehensive resource covers a variety of jazz topics, for beginners and pros of any instrument. The book serves as an encyclopedia for reference, a thorough methodology for the student, and a workbook for the classroom.
00311167 ....$18.95

JAZZ THEORY RESOURCES
by Bert Ligon
Houston Publishing, Inc.

This is a jazz theory text in two volumes. **Volume 1 includes:** review of basic theory • rhythm in jazz performance • triadic generalization • diatonic harmonic progressions and analysis • substitutions and turnarounds • and more. **Volume 2 includes:** modes and modal frameworks • quartal harmony • extended tertian structures and triadic superimposition • pentatonic applications • coloring "outside" the lines and beyond • and more.
00030458 Volume 1 ....$39.95
00030459 Volume 2 ....$29.95

JOY OF IMPROV
by Dave Frank and John Amaral

This book/CD course on improvisation for all instruments and all styles will help players develop monster musical skills! **Book One** imparts a solid basis in technique, rhythm, chord theory, ear training and improv concepts. **Book Two** explores more advanced chord voicings, chord arranging techniques and more challenging blues and melodic lines. The CD can be used as a listening and play-along tool.
00220005 Book 1 – Book/CD Pack $24.95
00220006 Book 2 – Book/CD Pack $24.95

THE PATH TO JAZZ IMPROVISATION
by Emile and Laura De Cosmo

This fascinating jazz instruction book offers an innovative, scholarly approach to the art of improvisation. It includes in-depth analysis and lessons about: cycle of fifths • diatonic cycle • overtone series • pentatonic scale • harmonic and melodic minor scale • polytonal order of keys • blues and bebop scales • modes • and more.
00310904 ....$14.95

THE SOURCE
THE DICTIONARY OF CONTEMPORARY AND TRADITIONAL SCALES
by Steve Barta

This book serves as an informative guide for people who are looking for good, solid information regarding scales, chords, and how they work together. It provides right and left hand fingerings for scales, chords, and complete inversions. Includes over 20 different scales, each written in all 12 keys.
00240885 ....$15.95

21 BEBOP EXERCISES
by Steve Rawlins

This book/CD pack is both a warm-up collection and a manual for bebop phrasing. Its tasty and sophisticated exercises will help you develop your proficiency with jazz interpretation. It concentrates on practice in all twelve keys – moving higher by half-step – to help develop dexterity and range. The companion CD includes all of the exercises in 12 keys.
00315341 Book/CD Pack $17.95

THE WOODSHEDDING SOURCE BOOK
by Emile De Cosmo

Rehearsing with this method daily will improve technique, reading ability, rhythmic and harmonic vocabulary, eye/finger coordination, endurance, range, theoretical knowledge, and listening skills – all of which lead to superior improvisational skills.
00842000 C Instruments $19.95

ARTIST TRANSCRIPTIONS

Artist Transcriptions are authentic, note-for-note transcriptions of today's hottest artists in jazz, pop and rock. These outstanding, accurate arrangements are in an easy-to-read format which includes all essential lines. Artist Transcriptions can be used to perform, sequence or for reference.

CLARINET

00672423	Buddy De Franco Collection	$19.95

FLUTE

00672379	Eric Dolphy Collection	$19.95
00672372	James Moody Collection – Sax and Flute	$19.95
00660108	James Newton – Improvising Flute	$14.95

GUITAR & BASS

00660113	The Guitar Style of George Benson	$14.95
00699072	Guitar Book of Pierre Bensusan	$29.95
00672331	Ron Carter – Acoustic Bass	$16.95
00672307	Stanley Clarke Collection	$19.95
00660115	Al Di Meola – Friday Night in San Francisco	$14.95
00604043	Al Di Meola – Music, Words, Pictures	$14.95
00673245	Jazz Style of Tal Farlow	$19.95
00672359	Bela Fleck and the Flecktones	$18.95
00699389	Jim Hall – Jazz Guitar Environments	$19.95
00699306	Jim Hall – Exploring Jazz Guitar	$19.95
00604049	Allan Holdsworth – Reaching for the Uncommon Chord	$14.95
00699215	Leo Kottke – Eight Songs	$14.95
00675536	Wes Montgomery – Guitar Transcriptions	$17.95
00672353	Joe Pass Collection	$18.95
00673216	John Patitucci	$16.95
00027083	Django Reinhardt Antholog	$14.95
00026711	Genius of Django Reinhardt	$10.95
00672374	Johnny Smith Guitar Solos	$16.95
00672320	Mark Whitfield	$19.95

PIANO & KEYBOARD

00672338	Monty Alexander Collection	$19.95
00672487	Monty Alexander Plays Standards	$19.95
00672318	Kenny Barron Collection	$22.95
00672520	Count Basie Collection	$19.95
00672364	Warren Bernhardt Collection	$19.95
00672439	Cyrus Chestnut Collection	$19.95
00673242	Billy Childs Collection	$19.95
00672300	Chick Corea – Paint the World	$12.95
00672537	Bill Evans at Town Hall	$16.95
00672425	Bill Evans – Piano Interpretations	$19.95
00672365	Bill Evans – Piano Standards	$19.95
00672510	Bill Evans Trio – Vol. 1: 1959-1961	$24.95
00672511	Bill Evans Trio – Vol. 2: 1962-1965	$24.95
00672512	Bill Evans Trio – Vol. 3: 1968-1974	$24.95
00672513	Bill Evans Trio – Vol. 4: 1979-1980	$24.95
00672381	Tommy Flanagan Collection	$24.99
00672492	Benny Goodman Collection	$16.95
00672486	Vince Guaraldi Collection	$19.95
00672419	Herbie Hancock Collection	$19.95
00672438	Hampton Hawes	$19.95

00672322	Ahmad Jamal Collection	$22.95
00672564	Best of Jeff Lorber	$17.99
00672476	Brad Mehldau Collection	$19.99
00672388	Best of Thelonious Monk	$19.95
00672389	Thelonious Monk Collection	$19.95
00672390	Thelonious Monk Plays Jazz Standards – Volume 1	$19.95
00672391	Thelonious Monk Plays Jazz Standards – Volume 2	$19.95
00672433	Jelly Roll Morton – The Piano Rolls	$12.95
00672553	Charlie Parker for Piano	$19.95
00672542	Oscar Peterson – Jazz Piano Solos	$16.95
00672544	Oscar Peterson – Originals	$9.95
00672532	Oscar Peterson – Plays Broadway	$19.95
00672531	Oscar Peterson – Plays Duke Ellington	$19.95
00672563	Oscar Peterson – A Royal Wedding Suite	$19.99
00672533	Oscar Peterson – Trios	$24.95
00672543	Oscar Peterson Trio – Canadiana Suite	$9.95
00672534	Very Best of Oscar Peterson	$22.95
00672371	Bud Powell Classics	$19.95
00672376	Bud Powell Collection	$19.95
00672437	André Previn Collection	$19.95
00672507	Gonzalo Rubalcaba Collection	$19.95
00672303	Horace Silver Collection	$19.95
00672316	Art Tatum Collection	$22.95
00672355	Art Tatum Solo Book	$19.95
00672357	Billy Taylor Collection	$24.95
00673215	McCoy Tyner	$16.95
00672321	Cedar Walton Collection	$19.95
00672519	Kenny Werner Collection	$19.95
00672434	Teddy Wilson Collection	$19.95

SAXOPHONE

00672566	The Mindi Abair Collection	$14.99
00673244	Julian "Cannonball" Adderley Collection	$19.95
00673237	Michael Brecker	$19.95
00672429	Michael Brecker Collection	$19.95
00672315	Benny Carter Plays Standards	$22.95
00672314	Benny Carter Collection	$22.95
00672394	James Carter Collection	$19.95
00672349	John Coltrane Plays Giant Steps	$19.95
00672529	John Coltrane – Giant Steps	$14.95
00672494	John Coltrane – A Love Supreme	$14.95
00672493	John Coltrane Plays "Coltrane Changes"	$19.95
00672453	John Coltrane Plays Standards	$19.95
00673233	John Coltrane Solos	$22.95
00672328	Paul Desmond Collection	$19.95
00672379	Eric Dolphy Collection	$19.95
00672530	Kenny Garrett Collection	$19.95
00699375	Stan Getz	$19.95
00672377	Stan Getz – Bossa Novas	$19.95
00672375	Stan Getz – Standards	$18.95
00673254	Great Tenor Sax Solos	$18.95

00672523	Coleman Hawkins Collection	$19.95
00673252	Joe Henderson – Selections from "Lush Life" & "So Near So Far"	$19.95
00672330	Best of Joe Henderson	$22.95
00673239	Best of Kenny G	$19.95
00673229	Kenny G – Breathless	$19.95
00672462	Kenny G – Classics in the Key of G	$19.95
00672485	Kenny G – Faith: A Holiday Album	$14.95
00672373	Kenny G – The Moment	$19.95
00672326	Joe Lovano Collection	$19.95
00672498	Jackie McLean Collection	$19.95
00672372	James Moody Collection – Sax and Flute	$19.95
00672416	Frank Morgan Collection	$19.95
00672539	Gerry Mulligan Collection	$19.95
00672352	Charlie Parker Collection	$19.95
00672561	Best of Sonny Rollins	$19.95
00672444	Sonny Rollins Collection	$19.95
00675000	David Sanborn Collection	$17.95
00672528	Bud Shank Collection	$19.95
00672491	New Best of Wayne Shorter	$19.95
00672550	The Sonny Stitt Collection	$19.95
00672350	Tenor Saxophone Standards	$18.95
00672567	The Best of Kim Waters	$17.99
00672524	Lester Young Collection	$19.95

TROMBONE

00672332	J.J. Johnson Collection	$19.95
00672489	Steve Turré Collection	$19.95

TRUMPET

00672557	Herb Alpert Collection	$14.99
00672480	Louis Armstrong Collection	$17.95
00672481	Louis Armstrong Plays Standards	$17.95
00672435	Chet Baker Collection	$19.95
00672556	Best of Chris Botti	$19.95
00672448	Miles Davis – Originals, Vol. 1	$19.95
00672451	Miles Davis – Originals, Vol. 2	$19.95
00672450	Miles Davis – Standards, Vol. 1	$19.95
00672449	Miles Davis – Standards, Vol. 2	$19.95
00672479	Dizzy Gillespie Collection	$19.95
00673214	Freddie Hubbard	$14.95
00672382	Tom Harrell – Jazz Trumpet	$19.95
00672363	Jazz Trumpet Solos	$9.95
00672506	Chuck Mangione Collection	$19.95
00672525	Arturo Sandoval – Trumpet Evolution	$19.95

FOR MORE INFORMATION, SEE YOUR LOCAL MUSIC DEALER, OR WRITE TO:

HAL•LEONARD® CORPORATION

7777 W. BLUEMOUND RD. P.O. BOX 13819 MILWAUKEE, WI 53213

Visit our web site for a complete listing of our titles with songlists at www.halleonard.com

0310